THE LAZARUS POEMS

HEINRICH HEINE

THE LAZARUS POEMS

With English versions

by

Alistair Elliot

MID NORTHUMBERLAND ARTS GROUP
in association with
CARCANET PRESS
1979

First published 1979
by Mid Northumberland Arts Group,
Wansbeck Square, Ashington, Northumberland
in association with Carcanet Press Limited
330-332 Corn Exchange Buildings, Manchester M4 3BG

Produced by computer-controlled phototypesetting using OCR
input techniques and printed offset by
Unwin Brothers Limited
The Gresham Press, Old Woking, Surrey
A member of the Staples Printing Group

In memory of my sister
Anne Dowling
1934–1975

and for her friends
in Germany

CONTENTS

INTRODUCTION

I

Heine lived in Paris nearly half his life, from April 1831 to his death in February 1856 at the age of fifty-eight. Many of his finest poems were written in this period of exile, and particularly in the last eight years, when he was bedridden and consciously dying of *tabes dorsalis*, a spinal degeneration which is now known to be a form of tertiary syphilis. There was no cure for this extremely painful disease, and Heine had to sleep—in fact, to live—on a heap of half-a-dozen mattresses piled on the floor, the 'mattress-grave' as he called it.

In spite of the illness, Heine's life continued to be sociable—though he was no longer able to move, as he had once been in the habit of doing, to escape visitors and tourists. His mind remained unaffected and he was witty and usually cheerful right to the end. His wife Mathilde (whom he had married in 1841 after they had been living together for years) must have been a main source of life and comfort to him, but Heine's biographers take very literally his repeated description of her as a child. She was a French country girl (from Normandy), illiterate and monolingual (Heine once said the only German she knew was 'Ich bin eine wilde Katze'—'I am a wild cat'), in short, a beautiful peasant, who shared so little of her husband's thought that she didn't even know he was a Jew.

Soon after the illness became serious enough to confine him to bed (he had been able to see something of the Paris revolution of February 1848 before the paralysis really set in, that May), Heine began to have great physical difficulty even in writing. He would compose in his head, often at night when sleepless, and dictate the verses in the morning. Such is the calm of these poems, it is hard to believe that they were written in those conditions, though they contain several allusions to the poet's awful handicaps. The reader just forgets, as Heine's visitors did, after the first shock of seeing his unrecognisably emaciated face, everything but the interest of what he has to say.

1

II

The poems collected here were originally published as two
separate cycles, and in different books. 'Lazarus', the first twenty
poems, appeared in Heine's verse book *Romanzero* (1851), in Part
II ('Lamentationen'); the eleven poems of 'Zum Lazarus'
('Additions to Lazarus') appeared in the poetry section ('Gedichte.
1853 und 1854') of his *Vermischte Schriften* ('Miscellaneous
writings'), volume 1, October 1854.

The Lazarus who presides over the poems is not the famous
brother of Martha and Mary whom Jesus brought back from the
grave and revived (*Gospel according to St John*, chapters 11 and
12), but the Lazarus who sat with his sores and his begging-bowl
at the rich man's gate and later went to heaven while the rich
man, 'Dives', went to hell (*Gospel according to St Luke*, chapter
16, verses 19-31). However, many of the poems have no reference
at all to those New Testament stories. Heine is using the name
Lazarus (which happened to have belonged also to one of his
maternal great-grandfathers) to help give unity and an appearance
of objectivity to poems which might otherwise have seemed
excessively personal. In a sense the poems are indeed 'about' his
own desire for life and his own difficulties (including lack of
money), but the persona of Lazarus is a useful device (among
others, like the matter-of-fact tone and the wilful contemporaneity)
to get rid of that taint of the merely egocentric which the first-
person poet (let alone the life-long political satirist) had always
avoided. Later Heine used the name of Lazarus again, in the
October-December 1854 issue of the *Revue des Deux Mondes*, to
cover a large mixed bag of translations of his recent verse. These
twenty-one pages (in prose) were called *Le Livre de Lazare*, and
they consisted of nineteen 'poems', one of them being the 'Zum
Lazarus' cycle (though re-titled 'Réminiscences' and with some
poems omitted). The translations were made by Saint-René
Taillandier under Heine's supervision, and it can hardly be
doubted that their general title means 'Poems of a modern
Lazarus'.

One other general indication of how to take the Lazarus poems
is provided by Heine in the *Vermischte Schriften* of 1854. Here, in

the prose section that precedes the poems (including the 'Zum Lazarus' cycle), Heine wrote of a young cleric afflicted with leprosy who in 1480 composed poems that became famous, though their author 'lived in a desert, hidden from everyone ... He sat miserable in his bleak wretchedness while all Germany triumphantly and jubilantly sang and whistled his songs.... Often in my sad night-visions I think I see before me the poor cleric of the Limburg chronicle, my brother in Apollo, and his suffering eyes peer with a strange fixity out of his hood; but in the same moment he slips past, and fading like the echo of a dream I hear the grating tone of the Lazarus-rattle.'

A cursory glance through the poems will show that they do not constitute a cycle in the modern sense of being in sections that could be individually complete but also carry forward a general story-line; on the other hand, they are not a haphazard collection. This is not the place for a long critical look at their arrangement, but, for example, the poem about Solomon ('Lazarus 10') might seem at first completely irrelevant to the cycle. However, a closer look shows that it is an expression, in decently indirect terms, of feelings that a paralysed husband must struggle daily to control; and that it is connected to the other poems through the prayer to the angels ('Lazarus 15') and the poem about the Last Judgement ('Lazarus 3'). Moreover there is a characteristically Heinean sidestep from the previous poem, with its wish for a last quiet love affair, to this statement of Solomon's need for the Shulamite (his partner in the *Song of Songs*); and the poems are verbally linked through the last words of one ('ohne Lärmen') and the first words of the other ('Verstummt ...'). Besides this, there is the thought that the pattern of reciprocal needs in the story of Lazarus and Dives is paralleled in the Shulamite/Solomon relationship—and that Heine had a millionaire uncle called Solomon Heine.

Doubtless the ingenious reader can work out links that Heine did not think of himself, but there is a technical point that would seem to show conclusively that these poems were not put together casually, but composed as a group: the twenty poems of 'Lazarus', so many of them in quatrains, are actually in eighteen different metres or rhyme-schemes; and there are five still further different arrangements in the eleven 'Zum Lazarus' poems. Such variety implies careful planning.

3

III

The German text here is taken from Hans Kaufmann's edition of Heine's *Werke und Briefe*, Aufbau-Verlag, Berlin, 1961, Band 2 (edited and with notes by Gotthard Erler).

My translations follow Heine's line-length and rhyme-schemes, but usually I have substituted iambics for trochaeics, and in the irregular metres have usually dropped Heine's extra syllables (which to our ears are always on the edge of doggerel), and I have altogether disregarded the German patterns of masculine and feminine rhymes, which are not a tool of the trade in English. Finally, I tried half-rhyme in a few poems, and gave up rhyme altogether in one.

All Heine's constraints were however accepted by Edgar Alfred Bowring, whose *Poems of Heine complete. Translated into the original metres* was first published in 1859, three years after Heine's death. I am grateful to Mr Bowring's versions for saving me from at least one misreading. It also gives me pleasure to express my debt to Peter Branscombe's admirable Penguin *Heine*, now unfortunately out of print: it was a truly critical selection of the poet, without which I might never have followed up the excitement initially promised by Robert Lowell's three imitations of late Heine poems.

LAZARUS

1851

1 Weltlauf

Hat man viel, so wird man bald
Noch viel mehr dazubekommen.
Wer nur wenig hat, dem wird
Auch das wenige genommen.

Wenn du aber gar nichts hast,
Ach, so lasse dich begraben —
Denn ein Recht zum Leben, Lump,
Haben nur, die etwas haben.

1   *The way of the world*

If you've got plenty, then you'll soon
    Be adding more to it.
If hardly anything, you'll lose
    Even that little bit.

But if you've got damn all, my friend,
    Well, let them bury you:
To have the right to live you have
    To have a thing or two.

2 *Rückschau*

Ich habe gerochen alle Gerüche
In dieser holden Erdenküche;
Was man genießen kann in der Welt,
Das hab ich genossen wie je ein Held!
Hab Kaffee getrunken, hab Kuchen gegessen,
Hab manche schöne Puppe besessen;
Trug seidne Westen, den feinsten Frack,
Mir klingelten auch Dukaten im Sack.
Wie Gellert ritt ich auf hohem Roß;
Ich hatte ein Haus, ich hatte ein Schloß.
Ich lag auf der grünen Wiese des Glücks,
Die Sonne grüßte goldigsten Blicks;
Ein Lorbeerkranz umschloß die Stirn,
Er duftete Träume mir ins Gehirn,
Träume von Rosen und ewigem Mai —
Es ward mir so selig zu Sinne dabei,
So dämmersüchtig, so sterbefaul —
Mir flogen gebratne Tauben ins Maul,
Und Englein kamen, und aus den Taschen
Sie zogen hervor Champagnerflaschen —
Das waren Visionen, Seifenblasen —
Sie platzten — Jetzt lieg ich auf feuchtem Rasen,
Die Glieder sind mir rheumatisch gelähmt,
Und meine Seele ist tief beschämt.
Ach, jede Lust, ach, jeden Genuß
Hab ich erkauft durch herben Verdruß;
Ich ward getränkt mit Bitternissen
Und grausam von den Wanzen gebissen;
Ich ward bedrängt von schwarzen Sorgen,
Ich mußte lügen, ich mußte borgen
Bei reichen Buben und alten Vetteln —
Ich glaube sogar, ich mußte betteln.
Jetzt bin ich müd' vom Rennen und Laufen,
Jetzt will ich mich im Grabe verschnaufen.
Lebt wohl! Dort oben, ihr christlichen Brüder,
Ja, das versteht sich, dort sehn wir uns wieder.

2   *Looking back*

I've sniffed the smells from every pot
Our charming earthly kitchen's got;
Whatever tastes were in the air
I have enjoyed a hero's share,
From slurping coffee and gâteaux
To collecting pretty dolls in rows:
Silk waistcoat, finest tails in France,
And sovereigns jingling in my pants;
Like Gellert, a high horse to ride;
A house, a palace on the side.
I lay in luck's green meadow once —
The sun beamed golden compliments —
Across my brow a laurel crown
Where fragrant dreams breezed up and down
Wafting of roses and endless May —
Where it was bliss for me to stay
Dead lazy, swoon-addicted, dreamy —
Where roasted pigs would fly to see me,
And cherubs landed in white flocks
Hauling champagne-flasks from their frocks.
Oh visions! Bubbles that have popped!
Now, on some damp lawn, laid — or propped —
My limbs go rheumaticky and lame,
And my mind is overcast with shame.
Each pleasure, every happiness,
I bought with bitter, crude distress.
I became soaked in acrid pain,
And horribly bitten by bugs again;
I was oppressed with black anxiety;
I had to lie; all my society
Was borrowing off rich crooks, old whores.
I even had to beg, of course.
Now I'm tired of running — and walking — around.
I shall take a breather underground.
Keep well! Up above, dear Christian brother,
Naturally, we'll be seeing each other.

3 Auferstehung

Posaunenruf erfüllt die Luft,
Und furchtbar schallt es wider;
Die Toten steigen aus der Gruft,
Und schütteln und rütteln die Glieder.

Was Beine hat, das trollt sich fort,
Es wallen die weißen Gestalten
Nach Josaphat, dem Sammelort,
Dort wird Gericht gehalten.

Als Freigraf sitzet Christus dort
In seiner Apostel Kreise.
Sie sind die Schöppen, ihr Spruch und Wort
Ist minniglich und weise.

Sie urteln nicht vermummten Gesichts;
Die Maske läßt jeder fallen
Am hellen Tage des Jüngsten Gerichts,
Wenn die Posaunen schallen.

Das ist zu Josaphat im Tal,
Da stehn die geladenen Scharen,
Und weil zu groß der Beklagten Zahl,
Wird hier summarisch verfahren.

Das Böcklein zur Linken, zur Rechten das Schaf,
Geschieden sind sie schnelle;
Der Himmel dem Schäfchen fromm und brav,
Dem geilen Bock die Hölle!

3   *Resurrection*

One trumpet call fills the whole sky,
    And fearful echoes ring.
The dead climb out of where they lie,
    Shaking and shivering.

Then off they trot, all that have feet;
    White shapes of pilgrims flit
To Jehosaphat, where they must meet:
    That's where the Court will sit.

Christ sits as Judge at this Assize,
    The Apostles by Him too.
The verdict's loving-kind and wise
    From His twelve good men and true.

No face is muffled as sentence is passed:
    For every mask is dropped
On cloudless Doomsday when the Last
    Trumpet's sound has stopped.

This is Jehosaphat-in-the-Dell,
    Where the summonsed spirits hover,
And because the accused are too many to tell,
    Their summary trial's soon over.

The goats to the left, the sheep to the right,
    They're sorted, quick and well:
Good pious sheep to heaven's height,
    Lascivious goats to hell.

4   *Sterbende*

Flogest aus nach Sonn' und Glück,
Nackt und schlecht kommst du zurück.
Deutsche Treue, deutsche Hemde,
Die verschleißt man in der Fremde.

Siehst sehr sterbebläßlich aus,
Doch getrost, du bist zu Haus.
Warm wie an dem Flackerherde
Liegt man in der deutschen Erde.

Mancher leider wurde lahm
Und nicht mehr nach Hause kam —
Streckt verlangend aus die Arme,
Daß der Herr sich sein erbarme!

4   *The dying*

Run away for luck and sun,
Come back naked and undone.
German shirts and German hearts
Get worn out in foreign parts.

Pale as death and worse than ill,
If you're home, there's comfort still.
Warm as by a flickering hearth
One can lie in German earth.

Many, off the beaten track,
Crippled, never can crawl back,
Stretch out longing arms and cry:
Pity, Lord, this misery.

5   *Lumpentum*

Die reichen Leute, die gewinnt
Man nur durch platte Schmeichelein —
Das Geld ist platt, mein liebes Kind,
Und will auch platt geschmeichelt sein.

Das Weihrauchfaß, das schwinge keck
Vor jedem göttlich goldnen Kalb;
Bet an im Staub, bet an im Dreck,
Vor allem aber lob nicht halb.

Das Brot ist teuer dieses Jahr,
Jedoch die schönsten Worte hat
Man noch umsonst — Besinge gar
Mäcenas' Hund, und friß dich satt!

5   *A world of crooks*

The only way the rich are won
Is flattery of the lowest kind —
As cash itself, my dearest one,
Is smoothed by hand and grows˙refined.

Swing incense-tubs, be brazen, higher,
Before these godlike golden calves;
Worship them in the dust and mire —
Above all, never praise by halves.

This year the price of bread's gone up,
And yet the finest words are still
Found free — so take Maecenas' pup,
Write it an ode — and eat your fill.

6   Erinnerung

Dem einen die Perle, dem andern die Truhe,
O Wilhelm Wisetzki, du starbest so fruhe —
Doch die Katze, die Katz' ist gerettet.

Der Balken brach, worauf er geklommen,
Da ist er im Wasser umgekommen —
Doch die Katze, die Katz' ist gerettet.

Wir folgten der Leiche, dem lieblichen Knaben,
Sie haben ihn unter Maiblumen begraben —
Doch die Katze, die Katz' ist gerettet.

Bist klug gewesen, du bist entronnen
Den Stürmen, hast früh ein Obdach gewonnen —
Doch die Katze, die Katz' ist gerettet.

Bist früh entronnen, bist klug gewesen,
Noch eh' du erkranktest, bist du genesen —
Doch die Katze, die Katz' ist gerettet.

Seit langen Jahren, wie oft, o Kleiner,
Mit Neid und Wehmut gedenk ich deiner —
Doch die Katze, die Katz' ist gerettet.

6   *Reminiscence*

Some get the jewels, others the casket.
Oh Wilhelm Wisetzki, you died so young —
   But the cat, the cat, was saved.

The rafter broke, he was climbing on:
That's how he fell and died in the stream —
   But the cat, the cat, was saved.

We followed the corpse of the charming boy;
They buried him under the flowering may —
   But the cat, the cat, was saved.

Oh, you were wise; you soon outran
Our storms; you found a refuge soon —
   But the cat, the cat, was saved.

You escaped so early, were wise so young;
Before you got ill, you were over it all —
   But the cat, the cat, was saved.

For many long years, how often, dear child,
Jealous and sad, I've thought of you —
   But the cat, the cat, was saved.

7 Unvollkommenheit

Nichts ist vollkommen hier auf dieser Welt.
Der Rose ist der Stachel beigesellt;
Ich glaube gar, die lieben holden Engel
Im Himmel droben sind nicht ohne Mängel.

Der Tulpe fehlt der Duft. Es heißt am Rhein:
Auch Ehrlich stahl einmal ein Ferkelschwein.
Hätte Lucretia sich nicht erstochen,
Sie wär vielleicht gekommen in die Wochen.

Häßliche Füße hat der stolze Pfau.
Uns kann die amüsant geistreichste Frau
Manchmal langweilen wie die Henriade
Voltaires, sogar wie Klopstocks Messiade.

Die bravste, klügste Kuh kein Spanisch weiß,
Wie Maßmann kein Latein — Der Marmorsteiß
Der Venus von Canova ist zu glatte,
Wie Maßmanns Nase viel zu ärschig platte.

Im süßen Lied ist oft ein saurer Reim,
Wie Bienenstachel steckt im Honigseim.
Am Fuß verwundbar war der Sohn der Thetis,
Und Alexander Dumas ist ein Metis.

Der strahlenreinste Stern am Himmelzelt,
Wenn er den Schnupfen kriegt, herunterfällt.
Der beste Äpfelwein schmeckt nach der Tonne,
Und schwarze Flecken sieht man in der Sonne.

Du bist, verehrte Frau, du selbst sogar
Nicht fehlerfrei, nicht aller Mängel bar.
Du schaust mich an — du fragst mich, was dir fehle?
Ein Busen, und im Busen eine Seele.

7   *Imperfection*

Nothing is perfect in this world. The rose
Keeps company with thorns, and I suppose
Even the angels in the highest places
Are not immaculate, though full of graces.

The tulip lacks a scent. Rhinelanders say
Honest John stole a sucking-pig one day.
If Lucrece hadn't stabbed herself so fast
She might have found she had a child at last.

The proudest peacock has disgusting feet.
The wittiest woman, though she's always sweet,
Can sometimes bore us — like the *Henriad*
(Voltaire) or Klopstock's epic (good, but bad).

The smartest cow's a flop at Spanish, dumb
As Massmann is at Latin. The stone bum
Of Canova's Venus has too much patina:
It glints like Massmann's arsy nose, though leaner.

A sweet song's often cracked by sour rhymes,
Like stings left in the honeycomb sometimes.
Achilles' ankle, we all know, was groggy,
And Dumas' father was an Afro-Froggy.

In heaven's vault the purest-beaming star
Drops down on us if it should get catarrh.
The finest cider savours of the tun.
And blackheads can be spotted on the sun.

Dear honoured lady, even you are not
Faultless, not free of every sort of blot.
You look at me; you ask: 'What's lacking here?'
A bosom — and a soul inside it, dear.

8   *Fromme Warnung*

Unsterbliche Seele, nimm dich in acht,
Daß du nicht Schaden leidest,
Wenn du aus dem Irdischen scheidest;
Es geht der Weg durch Tod und Nacht.

Am goldnen Tore der Hauptstadt des Lichts,
Da stehen die Gottessoldaten;
Sie fragen nach Werken und Taten,
Nach Namen und Amt fragt man hier nichts.

Am Eingang läßt der Pilger zurück
Die stäubigen drückenden Schuhe —
Kehr ein, hier findest du Ruhe,
Und weiche Pantoffeln und schöne Musik.

8   *Pious Warning*

Immortal soul, be on your guard
To suffer no mortal pain,
As you leave the earthly plane:
The way, through death and dark, is hard.

At the city of Light, by the golden gate
God's soldiers on parade
Ask what you did and made:
They don't ask Name or Rank or State.

At the entrance the pilgrim leaves behind
His dusty, pinching shoes:
This floor for slippers soft and loose,
Beautiful music, peace of mind.

9   *Der Abgekühlte*

Und ist man tot, so muß man lang
Im Grabe liegen; ich bin bang,
Ja, ich bin bang, das Auferstehen
Wird nicht so schnell vonstatten gehen.

Noch einmal, eh' mein Lebenslicht
Erlöschet, eh' mein Herze bricht —
Noch einmal möcht ich vor dem Sterben
Um Frauenhuld beseligt werben.

Und eine Blonde müßt es sein,
Mit Augen sanft wie Mondenschein —
Denn schlecht bekommen mir am Ende
Die wild brünetten Sonnenbrände.

Das junge Volk voll Lebenskraft
Will den Tumult der Leidenschaft,
Das ist ein Rasen, Schwören, Poltern
Und wechselseit'ges Seelenfoltern!

Unjung und nicht mehr ganz gesund,
Wie ich es bin zu dieser Stund',
Möcht ich noch einmal lieben, schwärmen
Und glücklich sein — doch ohne Lärmen.

9   *Gone cold*

And when you're dead you have to lie
Such ages in the grave. Well, I
Am worried that before they raise
Us up, there will be long delays.

Just once, before my spark stops winking
And heart begins its final pinking,
Once more I'd like, while I'm still human,
To court the favours of a woman.

And it must be a blonde, with eyes
As soft as moonlight makes the skies —
For in the end I cannot bear
Wild suntanned ladies with brown hair.

Young people crammed with vital force
Want passion turned up full, of course,
With all that racket, raving, swearing,
Mutual heart-rending and soul-tearing . . .

Not young — well into my third score —
And hardly healthy any more,
May I love once again, and be
Lucky in love — but quietly!

10   Salomo

Verstummt sind Pauken, Posaunen und Zinken.
An Salomos Lager Wache halten
Die schwertgegürteten Engelgestalten,
Sechstausend zur Rechten, sechstausend zur Linken.

Sie schützen den König vor träumendem Leide,
Und zieht er finster die Brauen zusammen,
Da fahren sogleich die stählernen Flammen,
Zwölftausend Schwerter, hervor aus der Scheide.

Doch wieder zurück in die Scheide fallen
Die Schwerter der Engel. Das nächtliche Grauen
Verschwindet, es glätten sich wieder die Brauen
Des Schläfers, und seine Lippen lallen:

„O Sulamith! das Reich ist mein Erbe,
Die Lande sind mir untertänig,
Bin über Juda und Israel König —
Doch liebst du mich nicht, so welk ich und sterbe."

10   *Solomon*

Drums, trumpets, bugles have gone quiet.
In Solomon's camp the night-watch guards
Are angel shapes, all wearing swords,
On the left six thousand, the same on the right.

They protect the King from pain in dreams,
And if he darkly knits his brows
In a flash twelve thousand sword-arms raise
Out of the sheaths their steely flames.

Then back in the sheaths the tall flames topple
As the angels see the nightly terror
Is passing off, the sleeper's forehead
Goes smooth, his lips begin to babble:

'O Shulamite, the throne is my
Heirloom, the lands are subject to me,
I'm King of Israel and Judah:
But if you don't love me I wither and die.'

11   Verlorene Wünsche

Von der Gleichheit der Gemütsart
Wechselseitig angezogen,
Waren wir einander immer
Mehr als uns bewußt gewogen.

Beide ehrlich und bescheiden,
Konnten wir uns leicht verstehen;
Worte waren überflüssig,
Brauchten uns nur anzusehen.

O wie sehnlich wünscht ich immer,
Daß ich bei dir bleiben könnte
Als der tapfre Waffenbruder
Eines Dolcefarniente.

Ja, mein liebster Wunsch war immer,
Daß ich immer bei dir bliebe!
Alles, was dir wohlgefiele,
Alles tät ich dir zuliebe.

Würde essen, was dir schmeckte,
Und die Schüssel gleich entfernen,
Die dir nicht behagt. Ich würde
Auch Zigarren rauchen lernen.

Manche polnische Geschichte,
Die dein Lachen immer weckte,
Wollt ich wieder dir erzählen
In Judäas Dialekte.

Ja, ich wollte zu dir kommen,
Nicht mehr in der Fremde schwärmen —
An dem Herde deines Glückes
Wollt ich meine Kniee wärmen.

11 Vain wishes

The likeness of our dispositions
Pushing us round to congruence,
We were becoming all the time
Better disposed than we could sense.

Both of us decent, modest people,
We understood each other well.
Words were superfluous: we needed
Only a mutual look to tell.

How passionately I always wished
I could have stayed there, standing by
Through a campaign of pleasant sloth,
Comrade in arms and gallantry.

Yes, that was always my first wish,
That I could always stay with you.
Everything that could delight you,
Everything, I'd gladly do.

I'd have, to eat, what you found tasty,
And any dish that didn't suit
Would be removed at once. I'd even
Learn to puff at a cheroot.

And all those ancient Polish jokes
It always made you laugh to hear,
I would have told you yet again
In the dialect of Judaea.

Oh yes, I wanted to come back,
Give up my foreign vagrancies,
And by the fire of your good fortune
I meant to flex and warm my knees.

Goldne Wünsche! Seifenblasen!
Sie zerrinnen wie mein Leben —
Ach, ich liege jetzt am Boden,
Kann mich nimmermehr erheben.

Und Ade! sie sind zerronnen,
Goldne Wünsche, süßes Hoffen!
Ach, zu tödlich war der Faustschlag,
Der mich just ins Herz getroffen.

Solid-gold wishes! Precious bubbles!
Which like my life went down the drain —
Now I'm left lying on the floor
Knowing I shan't get up again.

Goodbye! the glittering wishes burst,
The sweet hopes hazily depart.
It had the deadly force of fate,
That blow: it caught me on the heart.

12   Gedächtnisfeier

Keine Messe wird man singen,
Keinen Kadosch wird man sagen,
Nichts gesagt und nichts gesungen
Wird an meinen Sterbetagen.

Doch vielleicht an solchem Tage,
Wenn das Wetter schön und milde,
Geht spazieren auf Montmartre
Mit Paulinen Frau Mathilde.

Mit dem Kranz von Immortellen
Kommt sie, mir das Grab zu schmücken,
Und sie seufzet: „Pauvre homme!"
Feuchte Wehmut in den Blicken.

Leider wohn ich viel zu hoch,
Und ich habe meiner Süßen
Keinen Stuhl hier anzubieten;
Ach! sie schwankt mit müden Füßen.

Süßes, dickes Kind, du darfst
Nicht zu Fuß nach Hause gehen;
An dem Barrieregitter
Siehst du die Fiaker stehen.

12   *Anniversary*

Nobody will sing a mass,
And no kaddish will be said,
Nothing said and nothing sung
In the first days I am dead.

But perhaps some later day
When the weather's mild and clean,
Frau Mathilde will go walking
On Montmartre with Pauline,

With a crown of everlastings
Come to decorate and sigh
Pauvre homme! to my grave,
Sadness welling in her eye.

Pity, I live too high up
And I can't produce a seat
For my darling here. Oh, she's
Tottering on her tired feet.

Sweet, fat child, no, no, you mustn't
Think of walking home. Ah, wait:
There's a cab-rank — can you see? —
At the cemetery gate.

13 Wiedersehen

Die Geißblattlaube — Ein Sommerabend —
Wir saßen wieder wie eh'mals am Fenster —
Der Mond ging auf, belebend und labend —
Wir aber waren wie zwei Gespenster.

Zwölf Jahre schwanden, seitdem wir beisammen
Zum letzten Male hier gesessen;
Die zärtlichen Gluten, die großen Flammen,
Sie waren erloschen unterdessen.

Einsilbig saß ich. Die Plaudertasche,
Das Weib hingegen schürte beständig
Herum in der alten Liebesasche.
Jedoch kein Fünkchen ward wieder lebendig.

Und sie erzählte: wie sie die bösen
Gedanken bekämpft, eine lange Geschichte,
Wie wackelig schon ihre Tugend gewesen —
Ich machte dazu ein dummes Gesichte.

Als ich nach Hause ritt, da liefen
Die Bäume vorbei in der Mondenhelle,
Wie Geister. Wehmütige Stimmen riefen —
Doch ich und die Toten, wir ritten schnelle.

13   Meeting again

The honeysuckle — a summer evening —
We sat at the window as before.
The moon, enlivening and leavening,
Rose, but two ghosts was all we were.

Since we last sat together here,
Twelve years subsided into Time:
Affectionate embers, the whole great flare,
Extinguished in the interim.

I sat, laconic. She, loquacious,
The woman, poked and poked about
Persistently in the old love's ashes.
But not a spark was still alight.

She told a long tale — how she'd won
Her fight against bad thoughts — some fight!
How very shaky her virtue had been —
At which I kept my face quite straight.

As I rode home, the moonlit trees
Seemed in the brilliance to run past
Like spirits — a sense of mournful cries —
But we, the dead and I, ride fast.

14   Frau Sorge

In meines Glückes Sonnenglanz,
Da gaukelte fröhlich der Mückentanz.
Die lieben Freunde liebten mich
Und teilten mit mir brüderlich
Wohl meinen besten Braten
Und meinen letzten Dukaten.

Das Glück ist fort, der Beutel leer,
Und hab auch keine Freunde mehr;
Erloschen ist der Sonnenglanz,
Zerstoben ist der Mückentanz,
Die Freunde, so wie die Mücke,
Verschwinden mit dem Glücke.

An meinem Bett in der Winternacht
Als Wärterin die Sorge wacht.
Sie trägt eine weiße Unterjack',
Ein schwarzes Mützchen, und schnupft Tabak.
Die Dose knarrt so gräßlich,
Die Alte nickt so häßlich.

Mir träumt manchmal, gekommen sei
Zurück das Glück und der junge Mai
Und die Freundschaft und der Mückenschwarm —
Da knarrt die Dose — daß Gott erbarm,
Es platzt die Seifenblase —
Die Alte schneuzt die Nase.

14   *Mrs Worry*

In my lucky time of radiance
The midges juggled their light dance.
My dear friends, full of love, would make
Sure I got some of my best steak,
    Fraternally handing round
    Fair shares of my last pound.

Now luck's gone off, the wallet's flat,
The friends have disappeared like that —
My sunny days are up the spout,
The midges are sitting this one out:
    When luck has come and gone,
    Midges and friends pass on.

Beside my bed in the winter night
Worry, my nurse, sits bolt upright.
She wears a waistcoat of white stuff,
A black cap, always, and takes snuff.
    The snuffbox hinge creaks sadly,
    The old neck wobbles badly.

Sometimes I dream that luck's migrating
Back to me with a May of mating,
Midges in swarms and friends with purses —
The box creaks — Hope of heavenly mercies
    Pops like a bubble — The old one blows
    Her nicotine-stained nose.

15   An die Engel

Das ist der böse Thanatos,
Er kommt auf einem fahlen Roß;
Ich hör den Hufschlag, hör den Trab,
Der dunkle Reiter holt mich ab —
Er reißt mich fort, Mathilden soll ich lassen,
Oh, den Gedanken kann mein Herz nicht fassen!

Sie war mir Weib und Kind zugleich,
Und geh ich in das Schattenreich,
Wird Witwe sie und Waise sein!
Ich laß in dieser Welt allein
Das Weib, das Kind, das, trauend meinem Mute,
Sorglos und treu an meinem Herzen ruhte.

Ihr Engel in den Himmelshöhn,
Vernehmt mein Schluchzen und mein Flehn:
Beschützt, wenn ich im öden Grab,
Das Weib, das ich geliebet hab;
Seid Schild und Vögte eurem Ebenbilde,
Beschützt, beschirmt mein armes Kind, Mathilde.

Bei allen Tränen, die ihr je
Geweint um unser Menschenweh,
Beim Wort, das nur der Priester kennt
Und niemals ohne Schauder nennt,
Bei eurer eignen Schönheit, Huld und Milde,
Beschwör ich euch, ihr Engel, schützt Mathilde.

15   *To the angels*

That one is Death, the evil one.
The horse he rides is dun, is dun.
I hear his hoof-beat, trotting free;
That's the dark horseman coming for me.
He drags me off, my heart just can't believe
I've got to leave Mathilde, got to leave.

She was my wife, my child as well:
I'm going to Shadow-land, to Hell;
She'll be a widow-orphan then,
And here I'll leave alone again
The wife, the trustful child who learned to rest
Carefree till now and faithful on my breast.

O Angels high in heavenly airs,
Pick up my low and sobbing prayers:
After I'm dead and bleakly buried
Protect the wife I've loved and married.
Be guardians to your image — my Mathilde —
Protect my poor child, shelter her and shield her.

By all the tears you've ever shed
Over mankind's unhappy head,
By the Great Name that's known and said
Only by priests, and then with dread,
By your own beauty, graceful, pure and mild,
Angels, I beg, protect my wife-and-child.

16 Im Oktober 1849

Gelegt hat sich der starke Wind,
Und wieder stille wird's daheime;
Germania, das große Kind,
Erfreut sich wieder seiner Weihnachtsbäume.

Wir treiben jetzt Familienglück —
Was höher lockt, das ist vom Übel —
Die Friedensschwalbe kehrt zurück,
Die einst genistet in des Hauses Giebel.

Gemütlich ruhen Wald und Fluß,
Von sanftem Mondlicht übergossen;
Nur manchmal knallt's — Ist das ein Schuß? —
Es ist vielleicht ein Freund, den man erschossen.

Vielleicht mit Waffen in der Hand
Hat man den Tollkopf angetroffen
(Nicht jeder hat soviel Verstand
Wie Flaccus, der so kühn davongeloffen).

Es knallt. Es ist ein Fest vielleicht,
Ein Feuerwerk zur Goethefeier! —
Die Sontag, die dem Grab entsteigt,
Begrüßt Raketenlärm — die alte Leier.

Auch Liszt taucht wieder auf, der Franz,
Er lebt, er liegt nicht blutgerötet
Auf einem Schlachtfeld Ungarlands;
Kein Russe noch Kroat' hat ihn getötet.

Es fiel der Freiheit letzte Schanz',
Und Ungarn blutet sich zu Tode —
Doch unversehrt blieb Ritter Franz,
Sein Säbel auch — er liegt in der Kommode.

16   In October 1849

The strong wind has gone down, it's mild
At home again, and life's at ease:
Germania, that great big child,
Enjoys itself with thoughts of Christmas trees.

We're busy with domestic bliss —
What tempts you higher must be sin:
The swallow too returns with peace
To the house whose gable it once nested in.

A cosy calm on wood and stream
With moonlight softly poured all over.
Bangs now and then. A shot? A scream?
A friend that someone's shooting, or a lover?

Perhaps they caught the crazy fool
With weapons in his hand today.
Not everyone's as wise — or cool —
As Horace, who so boldly ran away.

More bangs. Perhaps the firework section
Of the centenary do for Goethe —
Or rockets for Sontag's resurrection —
We thought she'd died (those songs!) in 1830!

And Liszt's popped up; he's still around,
Young Franz, he's not laid out blood-red
On some Hungarian battleground.
No Russian or Croatian struck him dead.

The last redoubt of freedom fell
And Hungary bleeds to death, but Franz
Remained unharmed, his sword as well —
In the chest of drawers, under the underpants.

Er lebt, der Franz, und wird als Greis
Vom Ungarkriege Wunderdinge
Erzählen in der Enkel Kreis —
„So lag ich und so führt ich meine Klinge!"

Wenn ich den Namen Ungarn hör,
Wird mir das deutsche Wams zu enge,
Es braust darunter wie ein Meer,
Mir ist, als grüßten mich Trompetenklänge!

Es klirrt mir wieder im Gemüt
Die Heldensage, längst verklungen,
Das eisern wilde Kämpenlied —
Das Lied vom Untergang der Nibelungen.

Es ist dasselbe Heldenlos,
Es sind dieselben alten Mären,
Die Namen sind verändert bloß,
Doch sind's dieselben „Helden lobebären".

Es ist dasselbe Schicksal auch —
Wie stolz und frei die Fahnen fliegen,
Es muß der Held, nach altem Brauch,
Den tierisch rohen Mächten unterliegen.

Und diesmal hat der Ochse gar
Mit Bären einen Bund geschlossen —
Du fällst; doch tröste dich, Magyar,
Wir andre haben schlimmre Schmach genossen.

Anständ'ge Bestien sind es doch,
Die ganz honett dich überwunden;
Doch wir geraten in das Joch
Von Wölfen, Schweinen und gemeinen Hunden.

Yes, knightly Franz is doing fine;
His grandsons when he's grey will hear
Him shooting his Hungarian line —
'I lay like this; I stuck my sword in *here*!'

But at the name of Hungary
My German jacket gets too tight:
There's roaring in it like a sea,
And trumpets sounding, calling me to fight.

It calls back, clattering, to my brain
That savage, iron, heroic song,
Faded, but fading in again,
Upon the downfall of the Nibelung.

The subject's still heroic fate;
The ancient fabulous plot's the same;
The names are altered, and the date;
But still it's 'Heroes who have earned your fame'.

And it's the same relentless doom:
Though the proud banners float unfurled,
The heroes as foretold succumb
To the crude forces of the animal world.

This time the imperial Ox agreed
A contract with the Bear (& Whelps).
You fell — but cheer up, Magyar: we'd
A much worse shame to swallow — if that helps.

For you were beaten fair and square
By beasts heraldic, even fine:
While we wake up to find we bear
The yoke of wolves, ignoble dogs, and swine.

Das heult und bellt und grunzt — ich kann
Ertragen kaum den Duft der Sieger.
Doch still, Poet, das greift dich an —
Du bist so krank, und schweigen wäre klüger.

They howl, bark, grunt — I scarce endure
Their victory-smell, their victory-riot.
Hush, poet, that upsets you — you're
So ill, it would be better to keep quiet.

17   Böses Geträume

Im Traume war ich wieder jung und munter —
Es war das Landhaus hoch am Bergesrand,
Wettlaufend lief ich dort den Pfad hinunter,
Wettlaufend mit Ottilien Hand in Hand.

Wie das Persönchen fein formiert! Die süßen,
Meergrünen Augen zwinkern nixenhaft.
Sie steht so fest auf ihren kleinen Füßen,
Ein Bild von Zierlichkeit, vereint mit Kraft.

Der Ton der Stimme ist so treu und innig,
Man glaubt zu schaun bis in der Seele Grund;
Und alles, was sie spricht, ist klug und sinnig;
Wie eine Rosenknospe ist der Mund.

Es ist nicht Liebesweh, was mich beschleichet,
Ich schwärme nicht, ich bleibe bei Verstand; —
Doch wunderbar ihr Wesen mich erweichet,
Und heimlich bebend küß ich ihre Hand.

Ich glaub, am Ende brach ich eine Lilie,
Die gab ich ihr und sprach ganz laut dabei:
„Heirate mich und sei mein Weib, Ottilie,
Damit ich fromm wie du und glücklich sei."

Was sie zur Antwort gab, das weiß ich nimmer,
Denn ich erwachte jählings — und ich war
Wieder ein Kranker, der im Krankenzimmer
Trostlos daniederliegt seit manchem Jahr. — —

17   Bad Dream

In my dream I was young and quick again —
High on the mountain-edge the villa stands —
Racing along the path there I ran down
And down, racing Ottilie, holding hands.

That little shape, so finely formed! The sweet
Twinkle of sea-green eyes, the fairy face . . .
She stands so firmly on her little feet,
Image of strength combined with daintiness.

Her voice rings true: each feeling syllable
Appears a contour of her soul in sound,
And all she says is wise and sensible:
Words that the rosebud lips are lifted round.

Something steals over me — not lover's pain,
This isn't raving; I've still got my sense —
But marvellously her nature weakens mine,
And shivering secretly I kiss her hands.

I think at last I picked a lily, gave
Her it, then gave the message out loud too:
'Ottilie, marry me and be my wife,
So I'll be good and happy just like you.'

But what her answer was, I never heard —
For suddenly I woke, and I was here
Again, a sick man in a sick man's bed,
Laid up and hopeless, for the umpteenth year.

18   Sie erlischt

Der Vorhang fällt, das Stück ist aus,
Und Herrn und Damen gehn nach Haus.
Ob ihnen auch das Stück gefallen?
Ich glaub, ich hörte Beifall schallen.
Ein hochverehrtes Publikum
Beklatschte dankbar seinen Dichter.
Jetzt aber ist das Haus so stumm,
Und sind verschwunden Lust und Lichter.
Doch horch! ein schollernd schnöder Klang
Ertönt unfern der öden Bühne; —
Vielleicht, daß eine Saite sprang
An einer alten Violine.
Verdrießlich rascheln im Parterr'
Etwelche Ratten hin und her,
Und alles riecht nach ranz'gem Öle.
Die letzte Lampe ächzt und zischt
Verzweiflungsvoll, und sie erlischt.
Das arme Licht war meine Seele.

18 *It's going out*

The curtain falls; the play is done.
The ladies and the gents have gone.
And did they like it? Well, some paws,
I think, beat out some gloved applause.
A very worthy audience stood
And clapped its bard, with gratitude.
But now the building has gone dumb:
Light and delight give way to gloom.
Though listen: a mean wailing thud
Near the bare stage, in some dark place —
Perhaps the parting of a dud
String on an ancient double-bass —
And an ill-tempered rustling — that's
The stalls being searched by theatre rats.
It smells of oil-fumes, noisomely.
The last light moans and flaps about,
Desperately fizzing, and goes out.
That poor light was the last of me.

19 Vermächtnis

Nun mein Leben geht zu End',
Mach ich auch mein Testament;
Christlich will ich drin bedenken
Meine Feinde mit Geschenken.

Diese würd'gen, tugendfesten
Widersacher sollen erben
All mein Siechtum und Verderben,
Meine sämtlichen Gebresten.

Ich vermach euch die Koliken,
Die den Bauch wie Zangen zwicken,
Harnbeschwerden, die perfiden
Preußischen Hämorrhoiden.

Meine Krämpfe sollt ihr haben,
Speichelfluß und Gliederzucken,
Knochendarre in dem Rucken,
Lauter schöne Gottesgaben.

Kodizill zu dem Vermächtnis:
In Vergessenheit versenken
Soll der Herr eu'r Angedenken,
Er vertilge eu'r Gedächtnis.

19   *Last will and testament*

Now it's time to be a ghost,
Better get my will engrossed.
Like a Christian I'll devise
Presents for my enemies.

That respected opposition
Must inherit some fine day
All my sickness and decay,
My complete de-composition.

I bequeath you then the gripes
That inflate and pinch the tripes;
Simple pissing-pains; the wiles
Of perfidious Prussian piles.

You shall have my cramps and jerks,
Twitching limbs and running spittle,
Spine a kiln where bones burn brittle —
God the Giver's purest works.

Postscript to the inheritance:
The Lord shall dowse, when you have gone,
Your memory in oblivion,
And obliterate your monuments.

20   *Enfant perdu*

Verlorner Posten in dem Freiheitskriege,
Hielt ich seit dreißig Jahren treulich aus.
Ich kämpfe ohne Hoffnung, daß ich siege,
Ich wußte, nie komm ich gesund nach Haus.

Ich wachte Tag und Nacht — Ich konnt nicht schlafen,
Wie in dem Lagerzelt der Freunde Schar —
(Auch hielt das laute Schnarchen dieser Braven
Mich wach, wenn ich ein bißchen schlummrig war).

In jenen Nächten hat Langweil' ergriffen
Mich oft, auch Furcht — (nur Narren fürchten nichts) —
Sie zu verscheuchen, hab ich dann gepfiffen
Die frechen Reime eines Spottgedichts.

Ja, wachsam stand ich, das Gewehr im Arme,
Und nahte irgendein verdächt'ger Gauch,
So schoß ich gut und jagt ihm eine warme,
Brühwarme Kugel in den schnöden Bauch.

Mitunter freilich mocht es sich ereignen,
Daß solch ein schlechter Gauch gleichfalls sehr gut
Zu schießen wußte — ach, ich kann's nicht leugnen —
Die Wunden klaffen — es verströmt mein Blut.

Ein Posten ist vakant! — Die Wunden klaffen —
Der eine fällt, die andern rücken nach —
Doch fall ich unbesiegt, und meine Waffen
Sind nicht gebrochen — nur mein Herze brach.

20   Little boy lost

A misplaced sentry in the freedom-fight,
I held out loyally for thirty years,
Battling on without hope of winning it.
I knew I'd never reach home without scars.

I kept watch day and night. I couldn't sleep,
Unlike my comrades crowding in the tent —
Besides, the loud snores of that splendid troop
Kept me awake, when drowsy at the front.

Those nights, boredom got hold of me, and fear,
Often (only an idiot's not afraid):
To scare them off I'd whistle a rude air
With rhyming insults added in my head.

My rifle up, I stood on the alert
And if some fool came near, suspiciously,
I took good aim and served him up some hot,
Piping hot lead, straight into his vile belly.

From time to time of course it had to happen
These evil-minded fools were not so bad,
As shots, themselves. Indeed, the wounds are gaping,
I can't deny it, losing streams of blood.

Post for one sentry, vacant! The wounds gape —
If one falls, others come and close the rank.
I fall unbeaten; the weapons I give up
Are still not broken: only my heart broke.

ZUM LAZARUS

1854

1

Laß die heil'gen Parabolen,
Laß die frommen Hypothesen —
Suche die verdammten Fragen
Ohne Umschweif uns zu lösen.

Warum schleppt sich blutend, elend,
Unter Kreuzlast der Gerechte,
Während glücklich als ein Sieger
Trabt auf hohem Roß der Schlechte?

Woran liegt die Schuld? Ist etwa
Unser Herr nicht ganz allmächtig?
Oder treibt er selbst den Unfug?
Ach, das wäre niederträchtig.

Also fragen wir berständig,
Bis man uns mit einer Handvoll
Erde endlich stopft die Mäuler —
Aber ist das eine Antwort?

1

Scrap the holy parables,
Ditch the pi hypotheses —
And try solving these damned questions
Point-blank, no digressions, please.

Why do good men drag round bleeding,
Wretched with some heavy cross,
When, as gay as conquering heroes,
Villains trot on their high horse?

What's to blame? Perhaps our Lord's
Not almighty all this while?
Or does he produce this farce?
Christ, that would be really vile.

So we put our endless questions
Till some unknown with a handful
Of earth stops our craws at last.
That's supposed to be an answer?

2

Es hatte mein Haupt die schwarze Frau
Zärtlich ans Herz geschlossen;
Ach! meine Haare wurden grau,
Wo ihre Tränen geflossen.

Sie küßte mich lahm, sie küßte mich krank,
Sie küßte mir blind die Augen;
Das Mark aus meinem Rückgrat trank
Ihr Mund mit wildem Saugen.

Mein Leib ist jetzt eine Leichnam, worin
Der Geist ist eingekerkert —
Manchmal wird ihm unwirsch zu Sinn,
Er tobt und rast und berserkert.

Ohnmächtige Flüche! Dein schlimmster Fluch
Wird keine Fliege töten.
Ertrage die Schickung, und versuch,
Gelinde zu flennen, zu beten.

2

The dark dark lady held my head
To her heart that tender way.
But where her trickling tears were shed
My hair was streaked with grey.

She kissed me lame, she kissed me ill,
She kissed the sight from my eye;
She wildly mouthed my backbone till
She'd sucked the marrow dry.

My body's a corpse, a prison where
The ghost waits for the grave:
Sometimes it feels so grumpy there
It must run mad and rave.

Impotent curses! The most violent
Drives not one fly away.
Put up with fate: try to be silent
Whether you snivel or pray.

3

Wie langsam kriechet sie dahin,
Die Zeit, die schauderhafte Schnecke!
Ich aber, ganz bewegungslos
Blieb ich hier auf demselben Flecke.

In meine dunkle Zelle dringt
Kein Sonnenstrahl, kein Hoffnungsschimmer,
Ich weiß, nur mit der Kirchhofsgruft
Vertausch ich dies fatale Zimmer.

Vielleicht bin ich gestorben längst;
Es sind vielleicht nur Spukgestalten
Die Phantasien, die des Nachts
Im Hirn den bunten Umzug halten.

Es mögen wohl Gespenster sein,
Altheidnisch göttlichen Gelichters;
Sie wählen gern zum Tummelplatz
Den Schädel eines toten Dichters. —

Die schaurig süßen Orgia,
Das nächtlich tolle Geistertreiben,
Sucht des Poeten Leichenhand
Manchmal am Morgen aufzuschreiben.

3

How slowly it goes sneaking past,
Time, the creepy untouchable snail!
But I am stuck here motionless
On the same spot, as if in jail.

In my dark cell no ray of sun
Or gleam of hope strikes through the gloom:
I know I'll change these ghastly digs
Only for an unfurnished tomb.

Maybe I'm dead, died long ago:
Maybe it's ghosts, the other dead,
And not my fancies, that at night
Go gaily marching round my head.

It could indeed be apparitions
Of some divine old pagan sort —
They love to take dead poets' skulls
As grounds for their nocturnal sport.

These terrible sweet orgies, gangs
Of mad spooks having a good time,
The bard, with a cadaverous hand,
Tries to record next day in rhyme.

4

Einst sah ich viele Blumen blühen
An meinem Weg; jedoch zu faul,
Mich pflückend nieder zu bemühen,
Ritt ich vorbei auf stolzem Gaul.

Jetzt, wo ich todessiech und elend,
Jetzt, wo geschaufelt schon die Gruft,
Oft im Gedächtnis höhnend, quälend,
Spukt der verschmähten Blumen Duft.

Besonders eine feuergelbe
Viole brennt mir stets im Hirn.
Wie reut es mich, daß ich dieselbe
Nicht einst genoß, die tolle Dirn'.

Mein Trost ist: Lethes Wasser haben
Noch jetzt verloren nicht die Macht,
Das dumme Menschenherz zu laben
Mit des Vergessens süßer Nacht.

4

Once I saw lots of flowers blowing
Beside my path. Too idle though
To reach and pick them, I kept going
As my proud nag would have me go.

Now, wretched, deathly ill, just hours
From a grave dug and aired already —
The scent of those rejected flowers
Comes back and mocks me, haunting, heady.

And one flame-yellow violet,
Specially, burns often in my skull,
A raving beauty I regret
I never once enjoyed in full.

But Lethe is my comfort still,
The classic spa, whose waters can
With sweet forgetful darkness fill
And soothe the stupid heart of man.

5

Ich sah sie lachen, sah sie lächeln,
Ich sah sie ganz zugrunde gehn;
Ich hört ihr Weinen und ihr Röcheln,
Und habe ruhig zugesehn.

Leidtragend folgt ich ihren Särgen,
Und bis zum Kirchhof ging ich mit;
Hernach, ich will es nicht verbergen,
Speist ich zu Mittag mit App'tit.

Doch jetzt auf einmal mit Betrübnis
Denk ich der längstverstorbnen Schar;
Wie lodernd plötzliche Verliebnis
Stürmt's auf im Herzen wunderbar!

Besonders sind es Julchens Tränen,
Die im Gedächtnis rinnen mir;
Die Wehmut wird zu wildem Sehnen,
Und Tag und Nacht ruf ich nach ihr! — —

Oft kommt zu mir die tote Blume
Im Fiebertraum; alsdann zumut'
Ist mir, als böte sie postume
Gewährung meiner Liebesglut.

O zärtliches Phantom, umschließe
Mich fest und fester, deinen Mund,
Drück ihn auf meinen Mund — versüße
Die Bitternis der letzten Stund'!

5

I saw them laugh, I saw them smile,
I saw their whole lives fall apart;
I heard their cries, death-rattles, while
I looked on with an easy heart.

I walked behind their coffins too,
Right to the churchyard, dressed in black.
And then, I won't conceal from you
I took my lunch with some attack.

Now, all at once, I think with sadness
On the old crowd of long-dead forms:
As if in flares of amorous madness,
My heart turns over in strange storms.

It's Julia's tears that, bright and burning,
Run in my memory most of all;
The sorrow changes to wild yearning
And day and night it's her I call.

Often she comes in fever-dreams,
The dead flower, posthumously now
Granting my ardour, as it seems,
A licence life would not allow.

Oh hold me, tender ghostly lover,
Hold me with all your fading power:
Press your sweet mouth to mine and cover
The bitterness of my last hour!

6

Du warst ein blondes Jungfräulein, so artig,
So niedlich und so kühl — vergebens harrt ich
Der Stunde, wo dein Herze sich erschlösse
Und sich daraus Begeisterung ergösse —

Begeisterung für jene hohen Dinge,
Die zwar Verstand und Prosa achten g'ringe,
Für die jedoch die Edlen, Schönen, Guten
Auf dieser Erde schwärmen, leiden, bluten.

Am Strand des Rheins, wo Rebenhügel ragen,
Ergingen wir uns einst in Sommertagen.
Die Sonne lachte; aus den liebevollen
Kelchen der Blumen Wohlgerüche quollen.

Die Purpurnelken und die Rosen sandten
Uns rote Küsse, die wie Flammen brannten.
Im kümmerlichsten Gänseblümchen schien
Ein ideales Leben aufzublühn.

Du aber gingest ruhig neben mir,
Im weißen Atlaskleid, voll Zucht und Zier,
Als wie ein Mädchenbild gemalt von Netscher;
Ein Herzchen im Korsett wie 'n kleiner Gletscher.

6

You were all trim fair-haired virginity:
So well-brought-up, so cool, that helplessly
I fretted for your small heart to unlock
And inspiration gush as from a rock —

Those feelings with their high inspiring glow
That Prose and Reason always count so low,
For which the noble, beautiful and good
On this earth dream, suffer, and shed their blood.

Once we went walking where the vineyards climb
The slopes beside the Rhine, in summer time.
The sun laughed over us, and tender fumes
Poured from the open cups of lovely blooms.

The roses and the violet carnations
Blew us red kisses, catching conflagrations.
It seemed that in the humblest daisy there
An ideal life unfolded to the air.

But you walked on beside me without heeding
In your white satin, full of your good breeding,
Like a Netscher painting of a girl (in Munich):
With a heart-sized glacier underneath your tunic.

7

Vom Schöppenstuhle der Vernunft
Bist du vollständig freigesprochen;
Das Urteil sagt: „Die Kleine hat
Durch Tun und Reden nichts verbrochen."

Ja, stumm und tatlos standest du,
Als mich verzehrten tolle Flammen —
Du schürtest nich, du sprachst kein Wort,
Und doch muß dich mein Herz verdammen.

In meinen Träumen jede Nacht
Klagt eine Stimme, die bezichtet
Des bösen Willens dich und sagt,
Du habest mich zugrund' gerichtet.

Sie bringt Beweis und Zeugnis bei,
Sie schleppt ein Bündel von Urkunden;
Jedoch am Morgen, mit dem Traum,
Ist auch die Klägerin verschwunden.

Sie hat in meines Herzens Grund
Mit ihren Akten sich geflüchtet —
Nur eins bleibt im Gedächtnis mir,
Das ist: ich bin zugrund' gerichtet.

7

In front of Reason's jury-court
You're innocent: you've been acquitted.
The verdict says: there's no offence
Of word or deed this girl's committed.

Yes, you did nothing; you stood mute
While I was wasting in mad flame;
You didn't stir the fire; or speak;
And yet it's you my heart must blame.

And every night through all my dreams
A plaintive voice repeats its brief,
Accusing you of ill intent,
Saying it's you brought me to grief.

It calls up witnesses and proofs,
Drags heaps of archives round the place,
But in the morning, like the dream,
The plaintiff's gone, without a trace.

Papers and all, the poor soul's fled
Deep in my heart, to find relief.
But one thing in my mind's still clear —
And that is, that I've come to grief.

8

Ein Wetterstrahl, beleuchtend plötzlich
Des Abgrunds Nacht, war mir dein Brief;
Er zeigte blendend hell, wie tief
Mein Unglück ist, wie tief entsetzlich.

Selbst dich ergreift ein Mitgefühl!
Dich, die in meines Lebens Wildnis
So schweigsam standest, wie ein Bildnis,
Das marmorschön und marmorkühl.

O Gott, wie muß ich elend sein!
Denn sie sogar beginnt zu sprechen,
Aus ihrem Auge Tränen brechen,
Der Stein sogar erbarmt sich mein!

Erschüttert hat mich, was ich sah!
Auch du erbarm dich mein und spende
Die Ruhe mir, o Gott, und ende
Die schreckliche Tragödia.

8

Your letter came, a sudden lightning
That lit up my abyssal night,
Pointing how deep, to blinding light,
My misery is, how deeply frightening.

Now sympathy even finds a hold
On you! who in my desert just
Stood, silent as a portrait bust,
As marble-lovely, as stone-cold.

O God, how wretched I must be!
For even she begins to speak,
Tears break out on her stony cheek,
Even the granite pities me!

That vision shook me horribly.
O God, take pity on me too,
Bestow your peace upon me: you
Finish the hideous tragedy.

9

Die Gestalt der wahren Sphinx
Weicht nicht ab von der des Weibes;
Faselei ist jener Zusatz
Des betatzten Löwenleibes.

Todesdunkel ist das Rätsel
Dieser wahren Sphinx. Es hatte
Kein so schweres zu erraten
Frau Jokastens Sohn und Gatte.

Doch zum Glücke kennt sein eignes
Rätsel nicht das Frauenzimmer;
Spräch es aus das Lösungswort,
Fiele diese Welt in Trümmer.

9

The figure of the real Sphinx
Is like a woman's, not a Thing's —
That's guff about the paws and claws,
The lion's body, and the wings.

The riddle of this real Sphinx
Is dead obscure though. There were none
So hard among the ones unravelled
By Ms Jocasta's husband-son.

But luckily her riddle's not
Known to the female of our species:
If someone spoke the word that solves it,
This world of ours would fall to pieces.

10

Es sitzen am Kreuzweg drei Frauen,
Sie grinsen und spinnen,
Sie seufzen und sinnen;
Sie sind gar häßlich anzuschauen.

Die erste trägt den Rocken,
Sie dreht die Fäden,
Befeuchtet jeden;
Deshalb ist die Hängelippe so trocken.

Die zweite läßt tanzen die Spindel;
Das wirbelt im Kreise,
In drolliger Weise;
Die Augen der Alten sind rot wie Zindel.

Es hält die dritte Parze
In Händen die Schere,
Sie summt Miserere;
Die Nase ist spitz, drauf sitzt eine Warze.

O spute dich und zerschneide
Den Faden, den bösen,
Und laß mich genesen
Von diesem schrecklichen Lebensleide!

10

At the cross-roads sit the three,
Spinning and crying,
Thinking and sighing.
They are a nasty sight to see.

The distaff's held by the first:
She twists the twine
And wets each line —
That's why her hang-lip's dry with thirst.

The next lets the spindle wag.
Around it sways,
In comical ways,
And the old eyes droop in their red silk swag.

The third Fate, ready to clip,
Holds the shears with both thumbs;
Miserere she hums;
Her nose is sharp, with a wart at the tip.

O hurry up, slash the string
Of this foul mess.
Let me convalesce
From life's repulsive suffering.

11

Mich locken nicht die Himmelsauen
Im Paradies, im sel'gen Land;
Dort find ich keine schönre Frauen,
Als ich bereits auf Erden fand.

Kein Engel mit den feinsten Schwingen
Könnt mir ersetzen dort mein Weib;
Auf Wolken sitzend Psalmen singen,
Wär auch nicht just mein Zeitvertreib.

O Herr! ich glaub, es wär das beste,
Du ließest mich in dieser Welt;
Heil nur zuvor mein Leibgebreste,
Und sorge auch für etwas Geld.

Ich weiß, es ist voll Sünd' und Laster
Die Welt; jedoch ich bin einmal
Gewöhnt, auf diesem Erdpechpflaster
Zu schlendern durch das Jammertal.

Genieren wird das Weltgetreibe
Mich nie, denn selten geh ich aus;
In Schlafrock und Pantoffeln bleibe
Ich gern bei meiner Frau zu Haus.

Laß mich bei ihr! Hör ich sie schwätzen,
Trinkt meine Seele die Musik
Der holden Stimme mit Ergötzen.
So treu und ehrlich ist ihr Blick!

Gesundheit nur und Geldzulage
Verlang ich, Herr! O laß mich froh
Hinleben noch viel schöne Tage
Bei meiner Frau im statu quo!

11

The heavenly fields of Paradise,
The happy country, don't tempt me:
I'll find no women in the skies
Lovelier than the ones I see.

No angel with the finest wings
Could substitute there for my wife,
And sitting on a cloud to sing's
Not my choice for the eternal life.

O Lord, I think the best for me's
To leave me in this world, don't you?
But first, heal my infirmities,
And see about some money, too.

The world is full of vice and sin,
I know; I'm used to that, from years
Of pounding the macAdam in
This long and mucky vale of tears.

The hustling world won't get me down —
I hardly ever leave the house:
I like to stay in dressing-gown
And slippers, home, beside the spouse.

Leave me with her! My soul enjoys
So much the music I can hear
In the pure chatter of her voice!
And then her look, so true and clear!

Just good health, and a pay award,
That's all; just living here below
Happily ever after, Lord,
With my wife, in the status quo!

NOTES

The reader may be interested to know of George Eliot's essay on Heine (published only the month before his death) and Matthew Arnold's poem ('Heine's Grave') and essay (in *Essays in Criticism*, 1865). There are modern critical or biographical works on Heine by E.M. Butler, B. Fairley, S.S. Prawer and W. Rose, but there seems to be no detailed critical discussion of the 'Lazarus' poems in English, in spite of the generally expressed admiration of them.

Introduction: Heine called his bed the 'mattress-grave' (Matratzengruft) in the Nachwort to his book *Romanzero* (1851), in the first paragraph.

The poems omitted from the translations of the 'Zum Lazarus' cycle in the *Revue des Deux Mondes* were nos. 4, 9 and 10.

Lazarus 1: This poem is a paraphrase of 'For unto every one that hath shall be given, and he shall have abundance: but from him that hath not shall be taken away even that which he hath'—the moral of the parable of the talents (*Gospel according to St Matthew*, chapter 25, verse 29).

Lazarus 2: Gellert—an 18th century poet who when ill was given a horse by the Elector of Saxony.

Gebratne Tauben—a saying about the lucky ('roast pigeons fly into his mouth') which Heine is taking literally.

Lazarus 6: Heine has remembered his schoolfriend's name incorrectly: Fritz von Wizewsky.

Lazarus 9: Heine's wish for one more love affair was granted, in a very very quiet way, by his friendship with Elise Krinitz ('La Mouche'), in 1855.

Lazarus 10: The *Song of Solomon* mentions a guard of sixty valiant men (chapter 3, verses 7-8); the Shulamite occurs in chapter 6, verse 13.

Lazarus 11: Judäas Dialekte—Yiddish.

Lazarus 12: The Kaddish is a service recited in the synagogue specially by *orphan* mourners.

Montmartre—Heine is in fact buried in the Montmartre cemetery, and not all that far from the main street. But doubtless 'high' and 'here' mean 'in heaven'.

Lazarus 13: The last line contains a catch-phrase ('Die Toten ritten schnelle') from Bürger's ballad 'Lenore' (1773), in which a dead lover returns from the war on horseback and takes his fiancée for a midnight moonlit ride to his grave. 'Lenore' also has metrical connections with the next Lazarus poem, and thematic ones with Lazarus 15. It had recently been translated by Gérard de Nerval, who was a friend (and translator) of Heine.

Lazarus 16: 'Im Oktober 1849' doubtless has behind it the thought of the poet Sándor Petöfi's death on July 31st in the Hungarian rising.

The singer Henriette Sontag had just made a come-back after 19 years of retirement.

Heine (born Harry) is accusing Liszt (born Ferencz—hence the insistence on the Germanic form Franz) of not putting to use the ornamental sword he had been presented with in Budapest ten years earlier. 'here I lay, and thus I bore my point' are Falstaff's actual words (in prose, in *Henry IV Part I*, Act II, Scene 4). Heine is quoting Schlegel's translation word for word 'My German jacket'—Some of Heine's paternal ancestors had lived in Hungary.

'Helden lobebären' are among the opening words of the *Nibelungenlied*, which besides the well-known legendary part used by Wagner has a second, historical part about the overthrow of the Burgundian kingdom by the Huns.

'Ochse' means the emperor *Franz* Joseph's Austria, from which the Hungarians had been trying to free themselves.

Zum Lazarus 6: Netscher is a respected 17th century Dutch genre painter. Munich is not dragged in merely to make as awful a rhyme as Heine's; Heine spent a lot of time in art galleries there in his short period as a journalist in Munich (1827-28), and there is a famous girl-portrait by Netscher in one of them

Zum Lazarus 10: 'Zindel' commonly means taffeta—the German word is used of the cloth bought by Joseph of Arimathea to wrap Jesus's body in (*Gospel according to St Mark*, Chapter 15, verse 46); but it can also mean the same as 'Zinnober' (cinnabar, red mercury sulphide). I take it Heine is alluding to the texture and bright redness of the old women's eyelids, and have tried to include both meanings.

'Parze'—the Roman Parcae, the three Fates, who spin the threads of our lives, and cut them, with the abhorréd shears.